The Tangled Threads Of Existence

Words spun from the web of life

Sargun Kaur Chawla

BookLeaf Publishing
India | USA | UK

Made with ❤ on the BookLeaf Publishing Platform
www.bookleafpub.in
www.bookleafpub.com

Dedication

To my elder sister, Sarabjeet, for being my compass, always guiding me home and for all those who gazed out of the window, lost in thought and pondered at the vast expanse of life.

Preface

Poetry has always been a powerful tool for expressing emotions too convoluted to be described by mere words. The Tangled Threads of Existence is my attempt to capture various shades of life and stich them into intricate threads of poems reflecting the beauty of childhood, the murmurs of empathy and the passage of time and memories.

Acknowledgements

I would like to express my heartfelt gratitude to my family for their unwavering support and encouragement. To my elder sister, Sarab, who gave me my first novel and made me fall in love with the world of writing, fantasy and poetry, thank you for always taking out the time to read my poems and giving me your valuable insights. A special thanks to my English teacher, Mrs L.Greenwold for her constant motivation and belief in me.

I am also grateful to the Bookleaf publishing team for helping me publish my very first book to life.

Lastly, to you, dear reader, thank you for picking up this book and embarking on this voyage of emotions with me.

1. The Language of Tears

I asked my tear, "Why do you fall?"
And it replied, "When words fall short of expressing the depth of emotions,
The echoes of things mended and broken."

Some tears whisper grief,
Some blossom in the direst of conditions, bringing relief.
Some hold echoes of words left unsaid,
Others, a mirror that reflects regret.

Some, soothing lullabies of joy and happiness,
While others carry the burden of the soul's heaviness.
Some, the remnants of the ink of memories, both bitter and sweet,
Others, a river that cools the fire of defeat.

Some, the fragments of love,
Others, the scars of the hardest goodbye.

"Why do you glisten when you fall?" I asked.
It replied, "Even the blanket of night has patches of stars that shine,
And for a brief moment, even dawn and dusk intertwine."

2. The River That Knows My Name

The river calls to me in the night,
Its surface illuminated by the soft glow of moonlight.
And as I bend down to gaze,
It reflects the memory of a young face.

I see myself playing along the edge of the river,
It holds the fragments of laughter and a world devoid of fear.
It holds the echoes of whispered secrets and dreams,
And my younger mirror, who looks up at me and beams.

It carries the murmurs of a wish made under a shooting star,
Of naively trying to grasp things that seem so close and yet so far.
It resonates with the sound of the splash of the coin used to make a wish,
It cradles the ripples of the time of pure bliss.

I trace its path with my hands,
I don't ask how it remembers who I am and understands.
But a ghost of a smile lingers on my face,

Because there's a river that knows my name.

3. Tracing Back Childhood

Taking a walk down the lane,
When life was simply plain.
When we used to play in the rain,
When we believed ourselves to be Captain Jack Sparrow
And set off on treasure hunts.

When we used to jump from the last two steps of the stairs
And call it a stunt.
When we believed ourselves to be superheroes with powers,
When we used to wish under the shooting stars.

The canvas of childhood, painted with colors so bright—
We used to chase butterflies, our hearts filled with delight.
We used to soar up high, our kites,
We used to sit and talk underneath the old oak tree,
When we were just wild and free.

Chasing our imaginations, fantasies, and dreams,
When we used to climb trees and reach for the sky.
When we had our own imaginary world, where dreams could fly.

Tracing back childhood,
A journey through the heart's terrain,
Where every laugh, every smile, every tear
Leads us back to home again

4. The World Through Someone Else's Eyes

The inquisitive traveller steps inside the shop.
The chime of the bell announces his approach, and the owner of the shop lowers his newspaper, his eyes twinkling with wisdom and hope.

The traveller looks up at the endless lines of mirrors.
A mystical mist clings to the mirrors, clearing as he nears.

He curiously looks up at the mirror and sees
Not his own reflection, but something more profound and deep.

He sees an old man writing a letter to his wife,
Reminiscing about the joy they once shared in life,
The time they spent together when she was alive.

As he steps towards the next mirror, he glimpses
A soldier forced to extinguish the flame of another soldier's life,
While his face etched in regret.

Next, he sees a wealthy man piling up his fortune,

Yet, despite his riches, he remains upset.

He views a terminally ill patient,
Quietly enjoying the vast beauty of nature,
Unsure of his own future.

Lastly, he sees a child playing carefree,
Laughing and enjoying happiness and glee.

As he recedes back from the mirrors,
His own perception of life clears.

The owner looks up at him and smiles,
And says to the traveller, "Sometimes, all we need to do
is see the world through another's eyes."

5. A Conversation Between Life and Death

In a library not bound by time,
Where the books on the shelves gleam with a mystical shine,
Life and Death, its two scribes, closely follow behind.
Life searches for more blank books to find,
Murmuring to Death, "Why can't you try to be empathetic and kind?"

It replies, "It is not my fault that you fill the pages of the book in haste,
And then I have to close them back and encase the memories of a life someone once chased."
Life asks, "But how can a mortal spend their days when they have a constant fear of you lingering behind?"

Death replies, "I give a purpose to the soul as the scroll of their existence unwinds,
And attracted by the jewels of materialistic wealth, do some of them not forget to be compassionate and kind,
Leaving the boat of happiness and benevolence stranded in the sea, incapable of being found?"

Life answers back with a sad smile etched on its
immortal face,
“Some find meaning in the suffering and obstacles of life,
Others try to avoid the maze of the soul’s journey,
And severe their humanity, cutting it off like a flower
with a knife.”

And the library stood quietly, listening to their
whispered rifts.
It knew they both were crucial for life’s endless drifts.
The two were like darkness and light, both
complementing each other,
Incapable of thriving without one another

6. Echoes of Kindness and Empathy

Hello! I am looking for kindness and empathy.
They are missing if you see them, please tell them where I will be.
I have put up missing posters;
Tell them the world is getting colder.

Colder in kindness and empathy,
And just for show,
People wear a mask of sympathy.

Is it our inconsistency?
Did we actually forget our responsibility?
Perhaps we just overlooked it and went our separate ways.
Did kindness and empathy actually go astray?

Does it cost too much
To be the light in someone's darkest day?
To say two kind words and put a smile on someone's face?

Did humanity actually disappear?
Did we divulge too much into greed and fear?

Why do we humans treat everything as a race?
Why, instead of fighting, can't we just embrace?

Why can't we erase the past and turn over a new leaf?
Why, instead of fighting wars, can't we agitate for peace?

So, if you see kindness and empathy,
Please tell them where I will be.

7. Where Peace Lies

The sirens flare again,
Instead of clouds, the missiles pour rain.
Abu, a 5-year-old boy, scrambles to find a place to shelter himself from being slain.
After what feels like an hour or so,
He hears the sirens fade away.
He starts scanning the wreckage, looking for his dog, hoping to find him in the way.
And he sees people lying utterly still.
By now, he knows the drill.
He knows that they wouldn't wake up from their sleep.
When he was three, holding his parents' hands, he got confused when they started to weep.
And then he heard the sirens for the first time.
He didn't know that living happily was a crime.
In the blink of an eye, his parents were gone and he was all alone.
While living out in the streets, finding safe places to hide, he saw a small puppy all on its own.
He searched for its mother, but there was no one.
And one could say that they both were orphans of the war.
He picked it up and named him Peace.
He knew it meant harmony and freedom, for his mother

had told him so, and he kept it without a leash.
For this petrifying war was itself a leash,
Clinging too tightly on everyone, making it difficult to live and breathe.
They both became good friends,
And whatever morsels of food Abu could scrape to find,
he gave half of it to Peace, even though he was barely meeting ends.
He used to play with the other kids sometimes,
And if they fought at times,
They just said sorry and hugged each other, and everything became alright.
Abu pondered why adults cannot do the same and cease to fight.
Why fight in vain,
When it doesn't bring joy, rather more agony and pain?
He and Peace lived together,
And when a blast rang loud making Abu tremble with fear,
Peace would come up to him to wipe his tears.
A year passed, and the two stayed together.
Abu hoped that the mortifying situation would now be finally better.
His gaze lands on a white flag at a distance.
He knows that white means peace, for the people often prayed for its existence.
So he gets up from the bunker where he and his dog

Peace were hiding.
Peace trails behind him, and Abu steps out to see what's happening.
A shot fired strikes him down, and Peace starts crying,
Seeing Abu there lying.
As the world near it crumbled and swayed,
Abu's eyes became glassy and still.
Peace doesn't leave his side, unwavering in will,
And it lies down beside Abu.
Peace's fur gets soaked in red.
After a while, it closes its eyes.
Abu and peace lie in war's lap,
Becoming just another casuality in this grim mishap.
In the ashes of war, where dreams wither and die,
A boy and his dog whisper goodbye.

8. I Am Not a Beggar by Choice

As I was making my way through the clamour of the market one day,
Trying to evade the merciless gaze of the sunlight in May,
I saw an old man reading under the shade of a tree,
And though it was evident from his shabby and torn clothes that he was struggling on the streets,
Yet his brows were furrowed in concentration, and he was reading a book intently, seemingly unfazed by the relentless heat.

Curious, I went up to see.
His expression was etched with a lifetime's wisdom.
I asked him politely what he was so keenly reading.
Those wise and discerning eyes looked up at me, and he calmly replied, "Man's Search for Meaning."

As I struck up a conversation with him, he said, "I am not a beggar by choice."
A profound anguish was audible in his voice,
And he began to unravel his life's journey.
He said, "I was a professor of English, and words were the tools of my trade. I had a loving family—

My wife and my three-year-old daughter.
Our house was always filled with joy and laughter.
And on my anniversary, when I was going home with a rose in my hand for my wife,
War came over like a plague and took away my loved ones' lives.
I stood staring at the wreckage of my home,
And in a moment, I was all alone.
My city turned into dust right before my eyes,
The smoke of devastation and destruction filling up the skies."

With a hollow laugh, he said, "This world does not treat those kindly who stumble behind."
I saw a dried rose tucked between the pages of his book.
The man noticed my gaze and said,
"I could not give this to my wife, and now it is the only reminder I have of her and my daughter whom I left behind
Whom this war tore away and robbed of who they were happy, joyful, and kind."

I extended my hand to give him money,
But he shook his head and replied with a sad smile,
"My pursuit lies in knowledge, not coins."

9. A Conversation Between Life and Death

In a library not bound by time,
Where the books on the shelves gleam with a mystical shine,
Life and Death, its two scribes, closely follow behind.
Life searches for more blank books to find,
Murmuring to Death, "Why can't you try to be empathetic and kind?"

It replies, "It is not my fault that you fill the pages of the book in haste,
And then I have to close them back and encase the memories of a life someone once chased."
Life asks, "But how can a mortal spend their days when they have a constant fear of you lingering behind?"

Death replies, "I give a purpose to the soul as the scroll of their existence unwinds,
And attracted by the jewels of materialistic wealth, do some of them not forget to be compassionate and kind,
Leaving the boat of happiness and benevolence stranded in the sea, incapable of being found?"

Life answers back with a sad smile etched on its

immortal face,
"Some find meaning in the suffering and obstacles of life,
Others try to avoid the maze of the soul's journey,
And severe their humanity, cutting it off like a flower
with a knife."

And the library stood quietly, listening to their
whispered rifts.
It knew they both were crucial for life's endless drifts.
The two were like darkness and light, both
complementing each other,
Incapable of thriving without one another

10. The Stars That Wept for Earth

The stars watch the earth below,
Seeing it basking in the sun's eternal glow,
Flowers and plants—tiny murmurs of life—as they gently grow.
They see the shimmer of moonlight dancing on the waves of oceans and seas,
The forests whispering among themselves when they collide with a breeze,
The children playing under the shade of a tree.
They hear the echoes of their laughter, wild and free.

Occasionally, a star among them would graze the surface of the earth,
And they would smile when the people wished upon a shooting star, hoping for their wishes to be heard.
But as seasons change, fear and distress become evident in their eyes.
Instead of echoes of laughter and happiness, they hear the melancholic sound of cries.

They watch as the oceans carry the ashes of lives extinguished by wars,

How kindness flickers like the glow of a burning candle,
and their hearts clench as the earth silently roars.
They try to extend their hand to Earth, whom they love
and care for,
Wishing to help, but bound by invisible chains, silently
watching in despair.
The stars weep for Earth, watching in torment,
Unable to help the earth to mend.
Their light flickers as they grieve,
Unable to mend the earth or even offer words of relief.

11. The eternal nature of truth

The veil of darkness is insufficient to hold,
The radiance of truth that shines even from the blindfold.

It remains unseen in plain sight,
No gust of wind powerful enough to smother its light.

No matter how skilfully the web of lies is weaved,
Yet, at the end, the buried chest of truth is always
retrieved.

It burns like the everlasting flame of a candle;
Even the strongest foundation of lie is incapable to
handle
Its overwhelming burden, which eventually topples
down like a scandal.

One might perceive the sight of an oasis in a desert to be
real,
But his illusion is always shattered when he comes near.

The truth never fades; it patiently waits
For those bold enough to enter its gates.

12. The Last Goodbye

Cameras click, and a crowd gathers.
There's a family, all clad in white, whose world just shattered.
A coffin is in front of them, covered in tricolour.
The mother cries for the son she's lost.
The wife is silently staring at the cost her husband had to bear with his life,
Who didn't even get the chance to see his newborn daughter and his wife?

A soldier hands her a letter,
Numbly, she looks at it and traces her fingers over the name.
It's from the man who lost to life's cruel game.
She opens it up and reads,
As she reads, it feels as if her own heart bleeds.
It says, "In the hush of the dawn I stand,
Before the sun has cast its first ray.
I write these words which I long to say.
My heart is heavy yet filled with pride,
My duty is to my motherland; I cannot hide.

To my family, whom I hold so dear,
Your love vanquishes all my fear.

I don't know if it's the last time,
Not seeing my daughter is my only crime.
Please tell her I will be her father in my next lifetime.
Mother, please don't cry, for I serve my country on the battlefield,
Even if a bullet strikes me, my courage will not yield.
I only fight,
I only fight for my country's future so bright.

Through a stormy, gloomy night,
Your love is like a light,
Directing me towards home.
In the garden of your memories, I shall roam,
Until we meet again, in a world so high,
This is not the end of our story, just the last goodbye.

13. You Are Alive

When you feel like you have lost your way,
When you worry if the path of your life has gone astray,
When you look to the sky and question why,
When you feel shattered and you just want to scream,
When difficulties cloud the sky of your dream,
Remember that time too goes by,
And so will the difficulties clouding your sky.

Seasons too change and turn,
And through trials and rejection, you do not fail but you learn.
When you think that life is vain,
That it isn't worth the pain,
Remember the gentle breeze of the air
That caresses your hair.

Through triumphs and trials,
Remember the moments that made you smile
When you laughed with delight.
Even in the utter darkness of the night,
The stars defy all odds and shine bright.

In scars that whisper of past defeats,
There blooms a strength that none can beat.

You will achieve wisdom and grace,
For life is a lovely ever-changing place.
And when you think it's hard to survive,
You are reading this, you are alive.

14. The Gentle Promise of Time

Winter covers the surface of the earth like a veil,
When dark clouds prevail.
Sometimes, life is the same way—
There are times when problems might curtail,
A period of distress where everything seems lost,
When you might question, "Is it worth the cost?"

Fret not, for nothing lasts forever.
Just like the seasons pass, it gets better.
For after winter, spring prevails.

If winter covers the earth in a blanket of snow,
Then, in spring, the seeds of hope and happiness grow.
If storms rise and skies turn grey,
And you find yourself astray,
Remember, time—a benevolent healer—paves the way.

If you are in despair, you will surely find ease,
Just like autumn leaves in a gentle breeze.
Have faith in time, its steady hand,
As seasons change throughout the land.
If the sun sets, leaving the world in darkness,
It rises back again with double the brightness.

15. The Pursuit That Never Ends

Round and round, the hands of the clock move,
And we remain stuck in the same loop.
In the loop to prove ourselves the best,
Always chasing after worldly wealth without a moment's rest.

In our quest, we fail to see
The beauty of nature, wild and free.
And as the hours change into days,
We remain stuck in that same haze.

Wearing the blindfolds of unwavering belief,
That we are the ones who keep time on a leash.
We spend days and nights pondering over gaining more fame,
Trying our best to be the winner in life's game.

In our pursuit to glory, we never see
That time was never ours to keep.

16. The Dawn After Dusk

In the dark and daunting night,
When it feels there's no hope of finding the light,
When dreams seem so far away,
And courage begins to sway,

Don't be afraid of failure,
For there's beauty in falling with grace.
Life isn't always a race,

So, if you feel lost in a maze,
Remember, you are not truly lost,
For growth blooms best when storms have tossed.
So, dear reader, fret not if you cannot find your way—
Dusk may signal that one path is gone,
But it also paves the road for dawn.

Another day, a ray of hope,
Another chance to rise, to cope.
And when you think your efforts are in vain,
Find your strength and ignite your courage once again.

17. The Shadow of Greed

The shadow of greed silently lingers,
A presence that constantly whispers
To always strive for more—
A hunger that always roars.

It pours the spirit of temptation into a human's core,
Encouraging them to commit sins without any fear.
It keeps a human awake at night,
Trapping them into the veins of worldly wealth with its might.

It sets them off on a never-ending quest,
Diverging them to their worst and not their best.
Blinding their consciousness, putting them in a haze,
Trapping them in an endless maze.

It creates the illusion that they hold the vein of time,
Never realising that they are just mere puppets in greed's game—
All the while, they chase more fame.

18. What Happiness Might Be

If happiness was a colour, what would it be?
Would it be the earthy green of trees,
Or the rich, deep blue of seas?
For some, it’s the shimmer of moonlight—
For others, the sun's radiance shining bright.

If happiness had a voice, how would it sound?
Would it be the clapping when parents see their child
take those joyous first steps
Or the tears of relief echoing the soul's depths
Would it be the sound of laughter, wild and free?
Ultimately, happiness is however you perceive it to be.

19. The Prison of Expectations

They tell me it's alright,
As they hand me a perfect script to recite—
The role of my life already inked on the pages;
Who I'm, who I want to be,
Mentioned in the phrases.
They toss my dreams and expectations aside.

But what if I want something
else in life?
What if I wish to do something
That makes me feel alive?
What if I no longer want to
Be bound by expectations?
What if I no longer wish to
Strive for perfection?
What if I want to make
Mistakes and learn?
What if I truly wish to chase after
Something I fiercely yearn?
What if I no longer want to
Be a prisoner in this prison?
What if I no longer want to stay hidden?

20. The mirror's lies

Sometimes we gaze at the mirror, longing for perfection,
Frowning if we see a flaw in our reflection.
We look at the mirror and wonder how the world sees our face,
Chasing the allure of worldly charm—we remain lost in its haze.
Perhaps in our quest for perfection, we fail to recognise:
So let me tell you—the mirror lies.

A mirror doesn't reflect who we truly are;
It fails to see the depth of beauty that lies far.
It is unaware of the radiance of the soul;
It only shows a distorted image, not who we are as whole.
It only reflects the surface of who we are,
But there's beauty even in our scars.

21. A Conversation with the Skies

The philosopher asks the skies, "Where do you think happiness lies?"
It replies, "For some it lies in triumphs and victories,
For others, spending time with loved ones-when the heart is at ease.
Some feel the breeze of happiness by piling up the worldly wealth they gain,
Unaffected that in doing so they cause others pain.

The philosopher asks, "How do we ignite our strength again,
When we feel that our efforts are in vain?"
It replies, "The storm of darkness may growl with thunder,
But you cannot acquire wisdom without making a single blunder,
Don't be frightened of making mistakes,
For you will not feel the fresh air of success if you are in a haste.
When you stumble it gives you a chance to introspect and learn,

When you tried to take your first steps did you not
stumble innumerable times before you finally won?"

He asks, "How do we handle grief and loss"?
It replies, "The tides of sorrow may stretch far,
But you cannot overcome pain if you do not accept your scars".
The skies grew silent but the answers remained,
The philosopher smiled at the skies- thinking about the wisdom he gained.